BOOKS BY JOHN GABRIEL NAVARRA

CLOCKS, CALENDARS, AND CARROUSELS

FROM GENERATION TO GENERATION

OUR NOISY WORLD

A TURTLE IN THE HOUSE

WIDE WORLD WEATHER

THE WORLD YOU INHERIT

NATURE STRIKES BACK

FLYING TODAY AND TOMORROW

DRUGS AND MAN

WHEELS FOR KIDS

SAFE MOTORBOATING FOR KIDS

SUPERCARS

SUPERCARS

John Gabriel Navarra

SUPERCARS

A Chicago Museum of Science & Industry Book

DOUBLEDAY & COMPANY, INC., GARDEN CITY, NEW YORK

This book is part of a Museum of Science & Industry/Chicago series of science books published by Doubleday & Company, Inc. The series is designed to inform, stimulate, and challenge youngsters on a wide range of scientific and technological subjects.

Library of Congress Cataloging in Publication Data
Navarra, John Gabriel.
  Supercars.
  Summary: Describes some of the experimental cars being designed to deal with the present problems of automobile safety, air pollution, and gasoline shortage.
  1. Automobiles—Juvenile literature. [1. Automobiles] I. Title.
TL206.N38   629.22
ISBN 0-385-09381-0 Trade
      0-385-06827-1 Prebound
Library of Congress Catalog Card Number 73-10949

For every child who pleads to
sit on his father's lap and drive
—but especially for Johnny

1933 Chevrolet

1948 Chevrolet

1970 Chevrolet

Throughout the twentieth century each summer has been an important time for automakers. At this time of the year, after months of preparation, their new models are shown.

For more than seventy years the public has had a great interest in styling. And the automakers have been most obliging! The 1933 Chevrolet was boxy and squat. But by 1948 the Chevrolet was taking on new lines. And by the middle of the 1970s the Chevrolet Monte Carlo was publicized as a styling classic.

SHAPES CHANGE

THE SHAPE OF THINGS TO COME

Ralph Nader and others publicized the fact that many cars of the 1960s were unsafe at any speed. Today, people want to know about safety design and engineering. They are less likely to be attracted to sweeping lines and high styling unless safety is built in too.

A key feature of this four-door sedan is its roof. The roof is supported by a strong central pillar. This design allows the automaker to eliminate the front pillar. The wrap-around front window gives the driver better visibility.

There is an emphasis today on quality, safety, and design. People also want autos to have clean burning engines. If automakers work at it, we can have all four—styling, quality, safety, and clean air.

FAST IS THE WORD FOR IT

The Jaguar XJ12 sedan is equipped with air conditioning, automatic transmission, power brakes, power steering, and electrically operated windows. There is a huge 12-cylinder engine under its hood. Each cylinder produces a lot of power. This Jaguar will do 140 miles an hour.

Some people like powerful automobiles. But you cannot find many places where it is legal to drive a car above 70 miles an hour. In fact, safety experts tell us that we should be thinking about reducing speed limits on our superhighways and open roads.

Conservationists feel that powerful engines waste precious fuel. They want our local, state, and federal governments to levy new taxes on automobiles. They want these taxes to be based on the weight of the car and the horsepower produced by its engine. The conservationists believe that such taxes would discourage people from owning fast cars that waste fuel.

Triumph Spitfire 1500

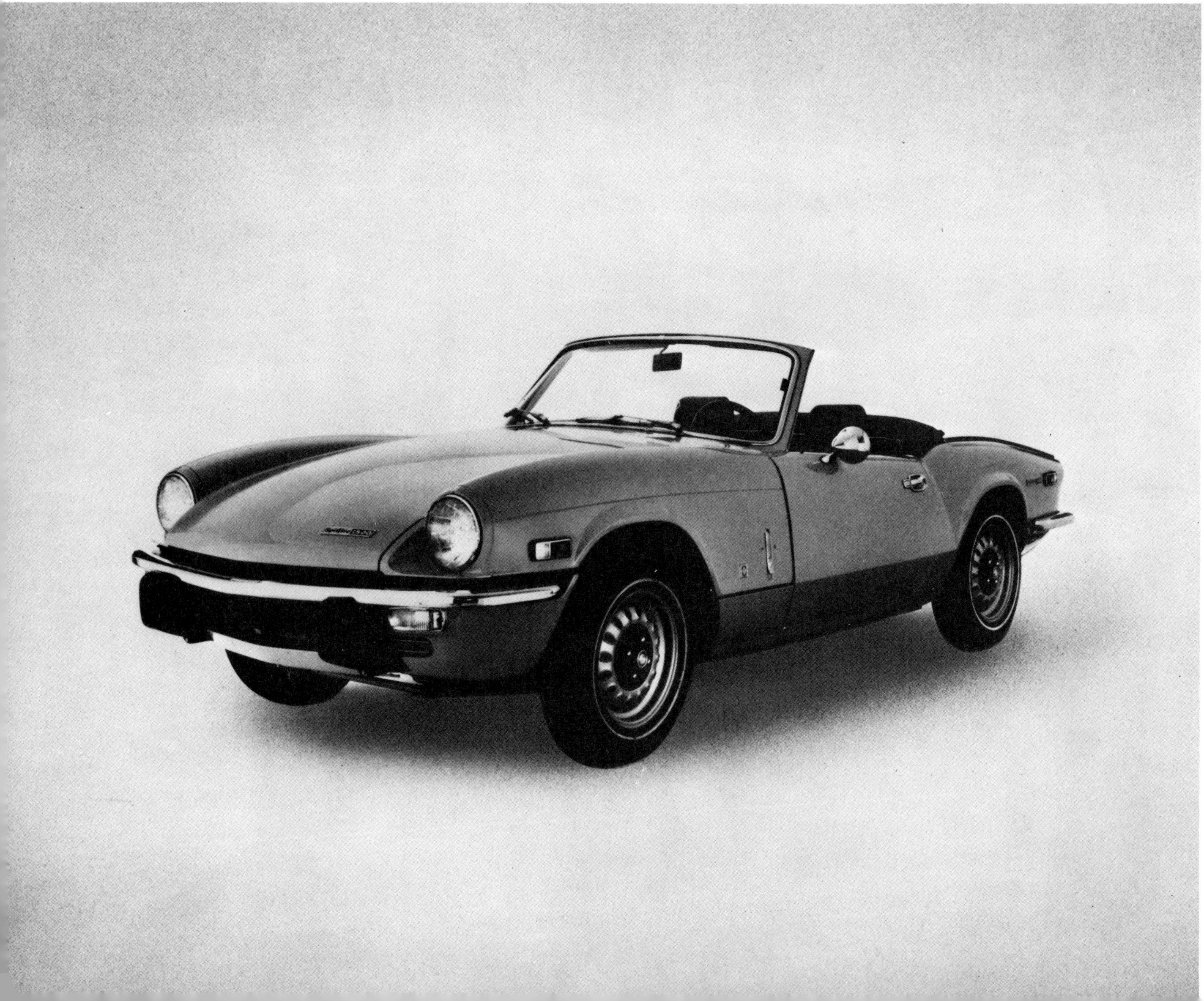

THE MIDGETS

The sales of small cars are running at record rates. In May 1973, 61 per cent of all the cars sold in the United States were subcompacts, compacts, or imports. Most of the imported models used 4-cylinder engines.

The Triumph Spitfire 1500 is a good example of a midget. It is a sports car that appeals to many people. In race after race, it comes in as a winner.

In 1973, the Ford Motor Company put into operation a new 4-cylinder engine plant. The 4-cylinder engines being produced by Ford are being used in the Pinto and the Mustang. The Ford Pinto is classified as a subcompact. The 1974 Mustang is a much smaller car than the Mustang Ford built in previous years.

The engine in the Fiat X1/9 is located in a compartment behind the seats. Because of the engine's position, the Fiat X1/9 is called a *mid-engine sports car*. There is an efficient use of space in this Fiat. There are luggage compartments at both ends.

Once the Fiat X1/9 is warmed up, it can be driven at a speed of 108 miles an hour. On a wet road it can accelerate from 0 to 60 miles an hour in 10 seconds. The engine location between the seats and the rear axle makes the car very stable.

Fiat X1/9

SAFER AND STURDIER

By 1974 there was no doubt about it! The automakers were attempting to make safer and sturdier cars. They put new emphasis on visibility. Bigger windows were installed in cars. There was also more emphasis on stronger bodies. Particular attention was given to the roof of the automobile. The goal was to make a roof that will not cave in.

In addition, 1974 marked the year that the first cars available for general sale were equipped with air bags instead of safety belts. The photo on the opposite page shows two bags being inflated. One bag is stored in the hub of the steering wheel. The other bag is stored behind the instrument panel. The bags become fully inflated in a fraction of a second when an accident occurs. In the photo on this page, you see the passengers moving forward into a pillow of air rather than the hard surface of the dashboard or the windshield.

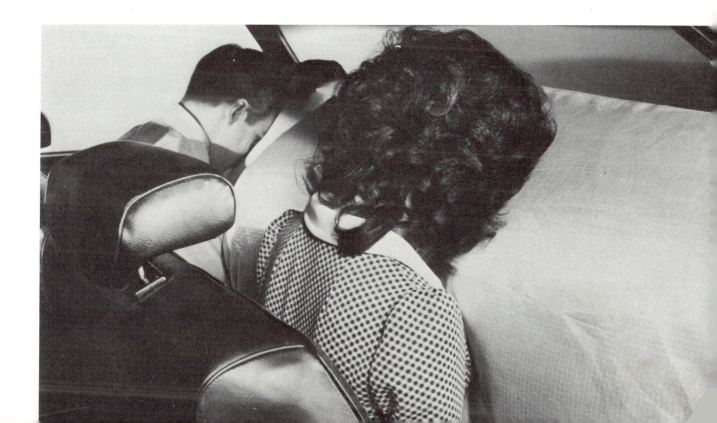

BUMPERS

Sturdier bumpers were built and placed on automobiles in the 1970s. And for the first time in 1974 all bumpers on all models were the same height. This means that the bumper height on a 1974 mini-car is the same as the height of the bumper on the largest 1974 limousine. The bumpers, in fact, were an eye-catching feature in the 1974 cars.

In 1974, the law stated that both front and rear bumpers must protect the car's "lighting, latches, and liquids" from all damage in collisions up to five miles an hour. Automakers approach the problem of complying with the law in different ways. Some companies, for example, use a plastic coating over their bumpers. Others use the traditional steel bumper and simply set it out from the body of the car. Some automakers, however, use hydraulic pistons which they mount between the bumper and the car frame. All of these systems are designed to absorb the shock of an impact.

Under the hood of the Daimler-Benz you can see the engine compartment. Notice the large crush zone between the engine compartment and the bumper. The crush zone is a safety area or buffer zone that serves to protect the engine. The bumpers on this car are designed to be energy absorbing too. There is a hydraulic piston mounted between the bumper and the frame of the car. When the bumper is struck, the hydraulic piston absorbs the energy of impact and protects the car from damage.

SAFETY BELTS

New safety-belt systems were introduced in 1974. The older system of separate lap and shoulder belts was replaced by a "three point" strap with a single buckle. The buckle in the system introduced in 1974 is connected electrically to the ignition system. This means that until the belt is fastened, the car cannot be started.

In fact, a special procedure must be followed to start a car that is equipped with the new safety-belt system: enter the car, buckle the belt, turn on the ignition. These three steps must be followed each time or the car will not start. If the belts are unbuckled after the car has been started, a dashboard light will flash and a buzzer will drone until the belts are rebuckled again.

In the photograph you see the well-padded interior of a Daimler-Benz. It has retracting seat belts that strap the front seat passengers in automatically. These seat belts, however, do permit some freedom of movement.

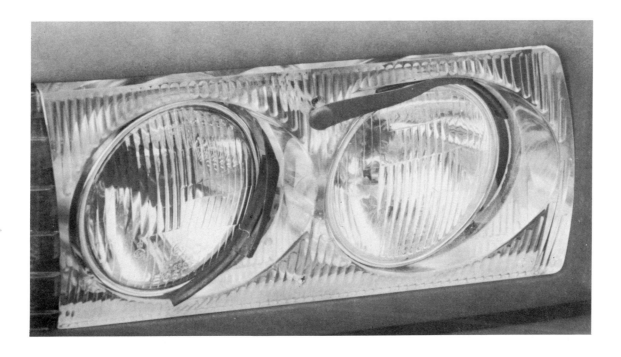

These headlights are equipped with wipers. A push on a button inside the car will cause water to squirt from the nipple below the lights. The same action sets the wipers in motion. In this way a driver can scrub dirt from the headlights while his car is in motion.

In the photo on the opposite page you can see a rear seat head-restraining net through the rear window. There is also a wiper for the rear window. The wiper is at the extreme right. The tail lights of the car have a corrugated effect. The corrugated design resists dirt build-up. Thus the tail lights will stay bright and not be dimmed by dirt. There is also an energy-absorbing bumper on this car.

AN EXPERIMENTAL SAFETY VEHICLE

In the photos you see the exterior and some of the interior of an experimental safety vehicle, the Nissan ESV. This four-passenger model was shown for the first time during Transpo '72 at Dulles International Airport, Washington, D.C.

This car has many safety features which are not yet on production models. For example, there is a rooftop periscope that provides three times as much rearward vision as a conventional mirror. And the interior of the car is made of noninflammable materials. The design of this model also insures passenger safety in a 50-mile-per-hour barrier crash.

The safety features built into this experimental vehicle are of two basic types: (1) features designed to help avoid accidents, and (2) features designed to help a person survive when an accident occurs.

Among the features that aid a driver in avoiding an accident are four-wheel disc brakes, an antiskid device, better vision and better lights, and safety tires that are used to keep the vehicle moving even if they are punctured. Among the features that serve to protect passengers in the event of an accident are a rigid passenger compartment, energy-absorbing front and rear ends, air bags, seat belts, and thick padding.

GASOLINE SHORTAGE

In 1973, motorists had something new to complain about. Refineries were unable to turn out enough gasoline to meet the booming demand.

The demand for gasoline in the United States increased by 6 per cent in 1972. The production of gasoline during that same year only increased by about 5 per cent. As you can see, production was not keeping up with demand.

In 1973 two things happened to further increase the demand for gasoline. First of all, a lot of new cars were bought. And each of the new automobiles was equipped with a pollution-control device. These devices actually increase the amount of gasoline needed to drive an automobile over a distance of one mile. Thus, the combination of a lot of new cars burning more fuel per mile created a demand for gasoline that could not be met.

After a fifteen-year lull, oil companies tell us that they once again are planning to build new refineries. This means that our ability to produce gasoline should catch up with the demand in two or three years.

In planning for the future, automakers are keeping one eye on the gasoline shortage and the other eye on the problems of pollution. The experimental special purpose car shown in the photo on this page is designed to carry two adults in front and two children facing the rear. This vehicle is being designed so that it can use gasoline, electric, or a combination of gasoline-electric power systems.

HYDROGEN CARS

There is no doubt that the world is facing a dwindling supply of natural gas, fuel oil, and gasoline. Some people are suggesting that we should turn away from these fossil fuels and begin using hydrogen.

Hydrogen is the lightest of all the elements. It is, in fact, one of the most abundant things we have on earth. Hydrogen can be produced by "pulling apart" the water molecule. Thus, hydrogen is available in large quantities wherever water exists.

When hydrogen is burned, it combines with the oxygen in the air to form water. This fact makes hydrogen a pollution-free fuel. It is also a recyclable fuel. We call hydrogen recyclable because man finds it in water and when hydrogen is burned it becomes water once again.

The car in the photo was designed by students at the University of California at Los Angeles. The auto has an internal-combustion engine that uses hydrogen instead of gasoline. Since hydrogen contains no carbon, the engine does not emit carbon monoxide or any other hydrocarbon.

There seems to be a lot of fumes coming out the exhaust pipe. But don't worry! That's steam you see coming out as exhaust gas. Steam is clean. It is not a pollutant.

THE CLEAN AIR ACT

The photograph on the opposite page was taken more than thirty years ago. The Ford Motor Company was introducing its 1940 models at the time. There were not too many automobiles on the roads of the United States in 1940. And the quality of our air was generally much better than it is today.

Air pollution has been a growing problem during most of the twentieth century. In 1970, the Congress of the United States took positive action and passed the Clean Air Act. The goal of Congress is straightforward: to bring air quality in the 28 major urban areas that house 30 per cent of the United States population within certain standards. Congress has set a time limit, too. They want our air to reach these standards by May 31, 1975.

The Congress of the United States feels that the automobile is a major source of urban air pollution. Thus the problem is what to do about the automobile. There are two suggestions: (1) purify emissions from cars and trucks, and (2) limit the concentration of vehicles in crowded urban areas where pollution is severe.

Hydrocarbons are chemical compounds made of two elements: hydrogen and carbon. Gasoline is a mixture of hydrocarbons. When a hydrocarbon is burned, each of its elements—hydrogen and carbon—combines with oxygen.

The complete combustion of carbon produces carbon dioxide. This is the same gas that plants use in the process of photosynthesis. When hydrogen combines with oxygen, it forms water. Thus, when we have complete combustion of gasoline we simply get carbon dioxide and water. These products are not harmful since both carbon dioxide and water are necessary for life.

In an internal-combustion engine, however, gasoline is not completely burned. Some unburned hydrocarbons are emitted from the exhaust pipe! In addition, carbon does not completely combine with oxygen to form carbon dioxide. When there is incomplete combustion of carbon, a dangerous gas called *carbon monoxide* is produced.

Another disadvantage to burning gasoline in an internal-combustion engine is that the engine operates at very high temperatures. The high temperature causes nitrogen in the air surrounding the engine to break down and react with oxygen. When nitrogen combines with oxygen it forms oxides of nitrogen.

Each of these pollutants, that is, unburned hydrocarbons, carbon monoxide, and oxides of nitrogen is harmful to plant life and animal life. The Clean Air Act of 1970 sets certain standards. The standards are set on the basis of how many grams of a pollutant are produced by a vehicle for each mile that it is driven.

The 1973 Honda engine met the 1975 standards. Honda's engine burns a lean mixture of gasoline and air to achieve more complete combustion of the gasoline.

Since a lean mixture of fuel cannot be ignited by a spark plug, Honda made a simple change in the internal-combustion engine. In the Honda engine, each spark plug is placed in a little chamber of its own above its cylinder. Then a rich mixture of fuel is sent to the spark plug chamber and a lean mixture is sent to the cylinder below. The term *stratified charge* is used to describe the fact that a rich mixture of fuel sits on top of a lean mixture. After the spark plug ignites the rich fuel mixture, the flame travels down into the cylinder and explodes the lean mixture.

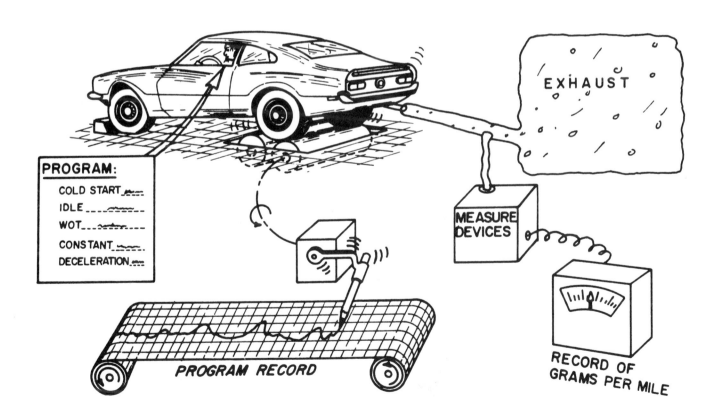

EXHAUST

PROGRAM:

COLD START

IDLE

WOT

CONSTANT

DECELERATION

MEASURE DEVICES

PROGRAM RECORD

RECORD OF GRAMS PER MILE

RESTRICT THE AUTO

There is no doubt that the automobile is a major source of urban air pollution. One solution to the problem is to ban the automobile completely from central cities. This, of course, loses sight of the fact that we have major highways running through most of our cities. In addition, we would be placing severe limitations on a person's freedom of movement.

The aerial view shows Lunalilo Freeway in the vicinity of Middle Street in Honolulu. The freeway has a lot of capacity. When the picture was taken, the freeway had very few cars on it. At certain times of the day, however, this freeway is choked with automobiles. And the traffic comes to a standstill!

The problem on most of our freeways is that they are enormously overloaded for about three or four hours each day. What can we do about it? Some traffic experts suggest that we may find it necessary to price freeway space. For example, if you want to use the freeway at 7:00 A.M., you may need to have a sticker on your car. A person would, of course, pay a certain fee for the sticker. Later in the day, however, a motorist would be able to travel on the freeway without a sticker.

CONTROL PARKING

Los Angeles and northern New Jersey, including the New York suburbs, will have the most difficulty in bringing air quality up to federal standards by 1975. Some experts say that the only way for Los Angeles to meet the standards is to ban all gasoline-powered vehicles.

One way to eliminate traffic is to eliminate on-street parking. Another way to discourage traffic is to limit the number of parking garages. Then motorists coming into an area will find fewer places to leave their cars. The inconvenience discourages people from driving cars into the city. And if all other remedies fail, parking fees can be increased so that it simply costs too much to bring a car into the area.

Each urban area has a problem. There is no single solution that will solve all of the problems. Each city must look to its own population and to its own business activity. Miami, for example, has established parking lots under the Interstate-95 Turnpike for the convenience of its motorists and tourists. Any solution should, of course, respect the rights of individuals as well as protect the quality of our air.

LITTLE CARS
FOR BIG CITIES

The automakers are attempting to come up with their own solutions to the urban problem. They, of course, do not wish to have the automobile banned from the inner city. Thus they are attempting to design congestion-fighters.

The "urban" car designed by the Ford Motor Company is especially made for shopping where parking is difficult. The car is suitable for two people. It can also carry a large amount of cargo. One of the features of this congestion-fighter is a wide door which allows easy entrance and exit. The car also has two hatches. These hatches allow the car to be loaded conveniently either at curbside or at the rear.

The prime concern of the cities, however, is the emissions that come from a car's engine. Most cities are indicating that they will have a regular procedure for inspecting car emission systems. This is a good way to fight pollution. This tells a motorist that he needs to keep his pollution-control system working properly. Regular inspection of all car and truck exhaust systems is a part of the plan of New York, Chicago, Philadelphia, and Pittsburgh.

POLLUTION-FREE

In 1970 Congress set air pollution standards that had to be met by 1975. The 1975 standards require that an automaker equip his cars with a "clean" engine.

The basic problem with the internal-combustion engine over the years has been that it is grossly inefficient. The average engine produced in the 1960s, for example, used only 16 per cent of the energy contained in a gallon of gasoline. Most of the rest was blown out the exhaust pipe as pollution.

Since 1970, automakers have been experimenting with a variety of ways to clean up the internal-combustion engine. Most of the internal-combustion engines produced in 1974, however, simply filtered pollutants. The filth was still produced. It simply was not allowed to escape into the air.

Most auto manufacturers are searching for alternatives to the piston-driven engine. As new engines are developed, they are placed in experimental cars and tested.

THE PISTON ENGINE

The Ford LTD in the photograph below is driven by a piston engine. The piston is a rod-shaped part that fits tightly into the cylinder. When an internal-combustion engine is running, the piston moves up and down in the cylinder. This LTD had eight cylinders in its engine.

A piston goes through four strokes. On the intake stroke, the piston begins moving down. As the piston moves down, the intake valve opens at the top of the cylinder. A mixture of air and gasoline vapor flows through the opening into the cylinder.

The second stroke of a piston is called the *compression stroke*. At the beginning of the compression stroke, the piston begins to move up. The intake valve closes. As the piston moves up into the cylinder, it squeezes and compresses the fuel mixture.

When the piston reaches the end of the compression stroke, the spark plug sends an electric spark into the fuel mixture. The spark causes the mixture to ignite and explode. Thus, at the beginning of ignition the piston begins to move down. The expanding gases in the cylinder push down on the piston.

In the diagram, you will note that a connecting rod hooks the piston to a crankshaft. The piston, as it moves down after ignition, turns the crankshaft. And the crankshaft turns the flywheel in the engine.

The fourth stroke of a piston is called the *exhaust stroke*. During the exhaust stroke the piston moves up into the cylinder again. As the piston moves up, an exhaust valve opens and waste gases are pushed through the opening.

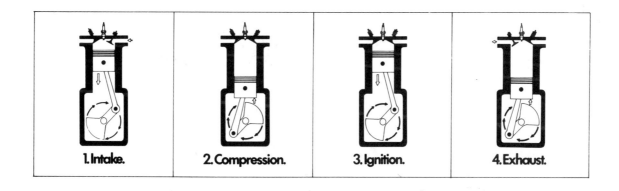

1. Intake.   2. Compression.   3. Ignition.   4. Exhaust.

THE ROTARY ENGINE

In 1973, the Mazda, a car with a rotary engine, rapidly gained popularity in the United States. The rotary engine is the invention of Felix Wankel. The first Wankel engines were developed in the 1950s.

The key to the rotary engine is a triangular-shaped rotor which revolves inside a chamber. Look at the chamber in the diagram on the opposite page. You will see that it looks like an oval which has been pinched at the sides. As each of the rotor's three sides makes a complete sweep of the chamber, it performs the same four "strokes" that a piston does in a piston-driven engine.

Look at the diagram marked *intake*. As the rotor tip passes the intake port in the chamber wall, the fuel mixture enters. There are no valves in the rotary engine. The gap between the side of the rotor and the chamber wall increases as the rotor continues to turn.

In the diagram marked *compression,* you will note that the next tip has passed the intake port. The fuel mixture is trapped between the leading rotor side and the chamber wall. As the rotor continues to turn on its not-quite-circular path, the fuel mixture is compressed.

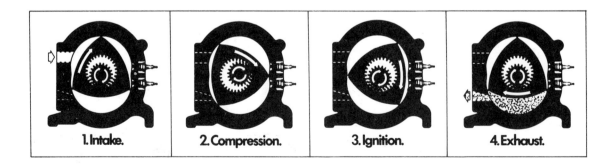

1. Intake. 2. Compression. 3. Ignition. 4. Exhaust.

In the diagram marked *ignition,* the fuel mixture is now compressed to about one ninth of its original volume. The rotor side is next to the spark plugs. The leading spark plug fires first. Then a split-second later the following plug fires to assure complete combustion of the fuel mixture. Once the fuel mixture is ignited, the gases begin to expand. The expanding gases drive the rotor along its path.

In the diagram marked *exhaust,* you see that the leading rotor tip has just passed the exhaust port. The gases, which are the products of combustion, are escaping from the chamber.

SIMPLICITY

It is understandable that people are enthusiastic about the Wankel engine. The smooth-running engine develops a lot of power. It is certainly quieter than the piston engine. The rotary engine is also more suitable to the task of turning the car's wheels than the jerky up-and-down motion of a piston engine.

There are three moving parts in the Mazda rotary engine. In the photo, you can see the simplicity of this new power plant's design. Two rotors are shown attached to the shaft. When ignition occurs, the power produced is transmitted directly to the shaft.

In this photo, you see the triangular-shaped rotor in its chamber. Note the position of the spark plugs. Once the rotor has made a complete revolution, the engine has completed the four-stroke cycle three times. The rotary engine produces about twice the horsepower of an ordinary piston engine of equal size and weight.

MEETING THE STANDARDS

The Wankel is, by nature, a dirty engine emitting its pollutants in the same way that the piston engine does. The Wankel, however, is small enough to leave much needed room under the hood for pollution-control equipment.

In 1973, the rotary engine used in the Mazda autos was able to meet the clean air standards of 1975. In order to meet these standards, the Mazda Company used several advanced pollution-control techniques.

Mazda used a fresh-air injection system. This system mixes oxygen with the raw exhaust gases. The exhaust gases mixed with the fresh air are then taken into a thermal reactor. Inside the thermal reactor the toxic hydrocarbons and carbon monoxide pollutants are heated along with the oxygen. The pollutants are thus oxidized to form water vapor and harmless carbon dioxide.

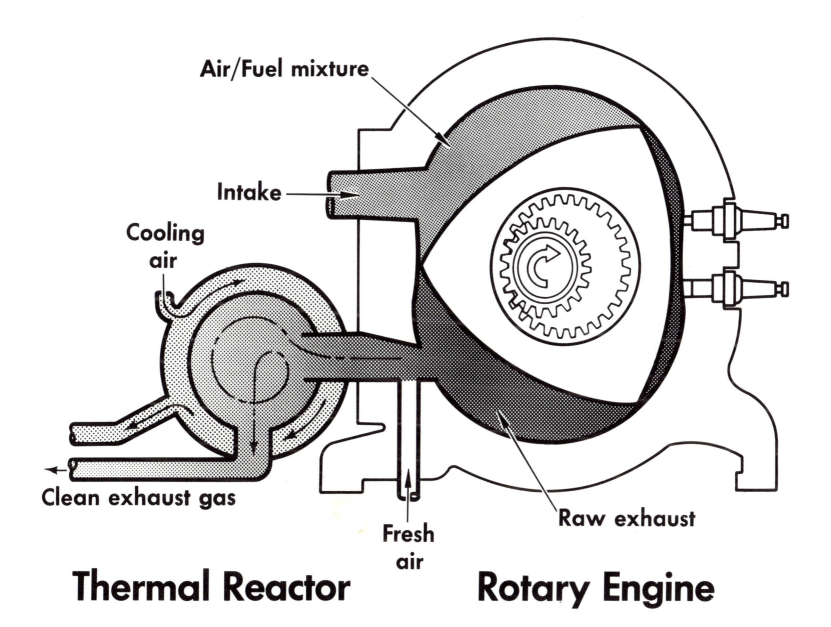

Air/Fuel mixture

Intake

Cooling air

Clean exhaust gas

Fresh air

Raw exhaust

Thermal Reactor

Rotary Engine

SOLAR-POWERED AUTO

This is an experimental car which went on world tour in 1960. It is the world's first solar-powered electric auto. There are over ten thousand solar cells mounted on top of this 1912 automobile.

The solar cells convert sunlight into electricity. The electricity produced by the sunlight is used to charge storage batteries. When the driver turns on the switch, the electricity is drawn from the storage batteries and is used to propel the car.

The idea for an electric car goes back to the beginning of the twentieth century. The solar cell, on the other hand, is a rather recent invention. It will take a blending of the old and new to solve some of the problems we are faced with today.

ELECTRIC CARS RETURN

The electric motor uses no fossil fuel. For all practical purposes, it runs silently. And, of course, there are much fewer moving parts in an electric car than in any other type.

Until a few years ago, however, large automakers did not seem to be interested in developing electric cars. The picture is changing rapidly. More and more people are spending more and more money on research in this area. The electric car, in fact, may be an ultimate solution to our problems of pollution.

The Comuta is an electric car built by the Ford Motor Company in Great Britain. There is room enough inside for two adults in front and two children in the rear. The top speed of the Comuta is 40 miles an hour.

The Mars II is an electric car developed by the Electric Fuel Propulsion Company. It is among the roomiest of the electric

vehicles. It has four lead-cobalt batteries and a system which uses braking energy to recharge the batteries. In other words, every time you apply the brakes in the Mars II, it helps to recharge the batteries. The top speed of the Mars II is 60 miles an hour. The range of the car is anywhere from 70 to 120 miles.

The principle of producing power by means of a turbine is very old. A windmill is an example of a simple turbine. It is driven by the air around it.

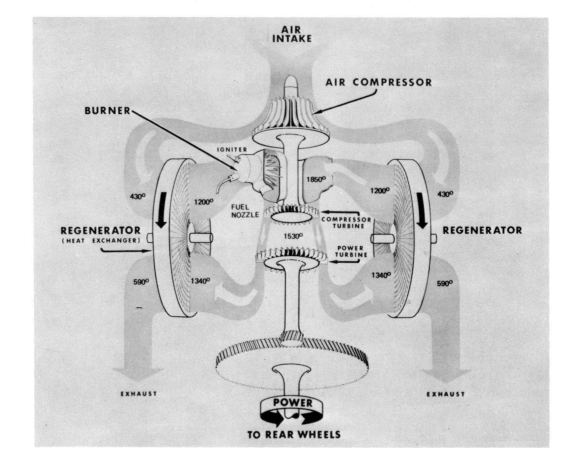

A turbine engine is designed to make its own wind. It does this by drawing air into the engine through a compressor. The air is heated in a burner to form a hot, rushing gas. The hot gas is then directed against turbine wheels. The spinning turbines transmit power through drive shafts to the vehicle itself. Follow the arrows which show the flow of air as it enters through the compressor until it is expelled as exhaust.

THE TURBINE CAR

Chrysler Corporation's turbine car is powered by a twin-regenerator gas turbine engine. There is, of course, no radiator. There are no pistons, no valve gear, and there is only a single spark plug for igniting the fuel in the combustion chamber.

THE STEAM TURBINE CAR

Since the 1960s, automakers have been thinking about steam engines. In theory, at least, steam power is clean and simple. A fluid, such as water, is heated until it vaporizes. The steam is vented from the boiler to a piston or turbine. The energy of the moving piston or turbine is then used to turn the wheels.

The steam engine is an external-combustion engine. A variety of liquids may be used as fuels. Diesel oil works quite well. In the photo, you see the world's first steam-powered car making its first test run on January 26, 1973, at Reno, Nevada.

This is a diagram of a Rankine cycle engine. It is similar to a steam engine, but it does not use water as a working fluid. Instead the Rankine engine uses an organic compound.

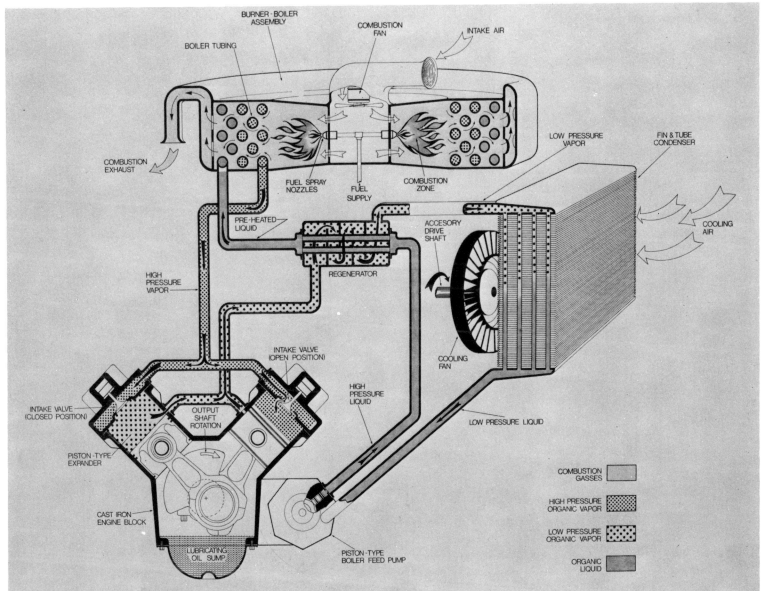

BURNER-BOILER ASSEMBLY

COMBUSTION FAN

INTAKE AIR

BOILER TUBING

LOW PRESSURE VAPOR

FIN & TUBE CONDENSER

COMBUSTION EXHAUST

FUEL SPRAY NOZZLES

FUEL SUPPLY

COMBUSTION ZONE

COOLING AIR

PRE-HEATED LIQUID

ACCESORY DRIVE SHAFT

HIGH PRESSURE VAPOR

REGENERATOR

COOLING FAN

INTAKE VALVE (OPEN POSITION)

HIGH PRESSURE LIQUID

LOW PRESSURE LIQUID

INTAKE VALVE (CLOSED POSITION)

OUTPUT SHAFT ROTATION

PISTON-TYPE EXPANDER

CAST IRON ENGINE BLOCK

LUBRICATING OIL SUMP

PISTON-TYPE BOILER FEED PUMP

COMBUSTION GASSES

HIGH PRESSURE ORGANIC VAPOR

LOW PRESSURE ORGANIC VAPOR

ORGANIC LIQUID

SPECIAL PURPOSE CARS

The car shown in the photograph is a small General Motors two-passenger vehicle. It is a lightweight car. Because it is lightweight, it requires less energy to propel it.

Special purpose cars are designed primarily for short-range urban transportation. They can also be used in light delivery service as well as for postal delivery service. Traffic experts tell us that such cars could be combined with a railroad system to provide intercity mass transportation.

The car in the photo is quite small, indeed. With its front wheels against the curb, the rear of the car would not extend beyond the width of a standard car. Three of these urban cars would fit in the same space as one regular-sized automobile.

Throughout the twentieth century, we have used general purpose automobiles. The special purpose urban car is a good idea. It may, however, mean rethinking some of our ideas about cities and transportation.

We do have a transportation problem in the United States. We are concerned about safety, the quality of our air, and the rapid depletion of our fossil fuels. The thing we must do is to agree as a nation on what we want to do. Then we must set about learning how to do it.

What do you think we want to do? How do you think we should go about doing it?

PHOTOGRAPHIC CREDITS

British Leyland Motors, pp. 13, 14, 28
Chrysler Corporation, pp. 56, 57
Electric Fuel Propulsion Co., pp. 55
Fiat, pp. 16, 17
Ford Motor Company, pp. 10, 32, 41, 44, 54
General Motors, pp. 8, 9, 18, 19, 29, 61
International Rectifier, pp. 52
Lear Motors, pp. 58
Mazda Motor Company, pp. 45, 46, 47, 48, 49, 51
Mercedes-Benz, pp. 4, 21, 22, 24, 25, 43
Nissan Motor Company, pp. 27
Thermo Electronic Corporation, pp. 35, 60
U.S. Department of Transportation, pp. 36, 59
UCLA, Tom Tugend, pp. 31

JOHN GABRIEL NAVARRA, the author of *Supercars,* is professor of geoscience and was, for ten years, chairman of the division of science at Jersey City State College. As both a teacher and a writer, Dr. Navarra has an international reputation. He was the teacher of the first televised science course to be offered in the South when he was on the faculty of East Carolina University. He has written a number of trade books for young readers as well as adult science books, and is the senior author of a complete series of science textbooks, grades kindergarten through nine, that are used by millions of school children throughout the United States.